# Exploring Solids And Boxes

## 3-D GEOMETRY

**TERC**

**Investigations in Number, Data, and Space®**

**Dale Seymour Publications®**

Menlo Park, California

The *Investigations* curriculum was developed at TERC (formerly
Technical Education Research Centers) in collaboration with Kent State
University and the State University of New York at Buffalo. The work was
supported in part by National Science Foundation Grant No. ESI-9050210.
TERC is a nonprofit company working to improve mathematics and science
education. TERC is located at 2067 Massachusetts Avenue, Cambridge,
MA 02140.

This project was supported, in part,
by the
**National Science Foundation**
Opinions expressed are those of the authors
and not necessarily those of the Foundation

Managing Editor: Catherine Anderson

Series Editor: Beverly Cory

Manuscript Editor: Karen Becker

ESL Consultant: Nancy Sokol Green

Production/Manufacturing Director: Janet Yearian

Production/Manufacturing Coordinator: Barbara Atmore

Design Manager: Jeff Kelly

Design: Don Taka

Illustrations: DJ Simison, Carl Yoshihara

Composition: Archetype Book Composition

This book is published by Dale Seymour Publications®, an imprint of
Addison Wesley Longman, Inc.

Dale Seymour Publications
2725 Sand Hill Road
Menlo Park, CA 94025
Customer Service: 800-872-1100

Order number DS43860
ISBN 1-57232-713-8
1 2 3 4 5 6 7 8 9 10-ML-01 00 99 98 97

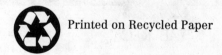
Printed on Recycled Paper

# Contents

---

\*Repeated-use sheet

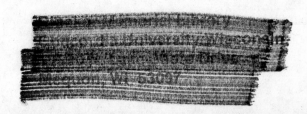

*Repeated-use sheet

# Identifying Geometric Shapes in the Real World (page 1 of 3)

## Geometric Shapes

## Real-World Objects

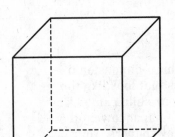

cube

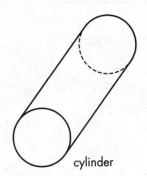

cylinder

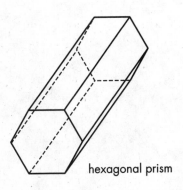

hexagonal prism

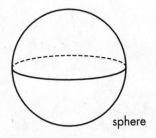

sphere

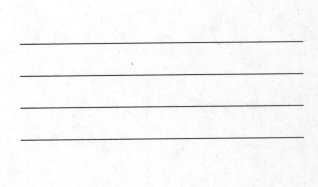

# To the Family

## Identifying Geometric Shapes in the Real World
*Session 1*

**Math Content**
Identifying three-dimensional shapes in the real world

**Materials**
Student Sheet 1
Pencil
Magazines, catalogs, newspapers (optional)

In class, we have been exploring and sorting a set of three-dimensional shapes. For homework, your child will find real objects that look like the solid geometric shapes pictured on Student Sheet 1. Your child can look for examples in and around your house (for example, a paper towel tube is a cylinder), as well as in magazines, catalogs, and newspapers. Your child will cut out or sketch examples and bring them to school.

# Identifying Geometric Shapes
## in the Real World (page 2 of 3)

Geometric Shapes

Real-World Objects

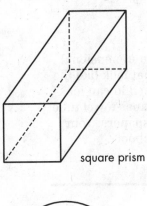

square prism

hemisphere

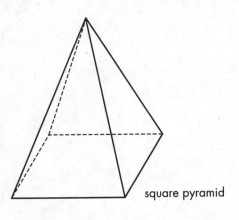

square pyramid

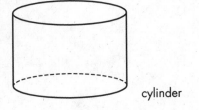

cylinder

_____

_____

_____

_____

_____

_____

_____

_____

_____

_____

_____

_____

_____

_____

_____

_____

_____

_____

_____

# To the Family

## Identifying Geometric Shapes in the Real World

*Session 1*

**Math Content**
Identifying three-dimensional shapes in the real world

**Materials**
Student Sheet 1
Pencil
Magazines, catalogs, newspapers (optional)

In class, we have been exploring and sorting a set of three-dimensional shapes. For homework, your child will find real objects that look like the solid geometric shapes pictured on Student Sheet 1. Your child can look for examples in and around your house (for example, a paper towel tube is a cylinder), as well as in magazines, catalogs, and newspapers. Your child will cut out or sketch examples and bring them to school.

# Identifying Geometric Shapes in the Real World (page 3 of 3)

## Geometric Shapes

## Real-World Objects

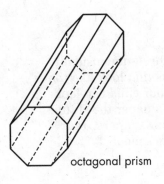

octagonal prism

_____

_____

_____

_____

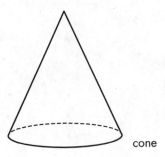

cone

_____

_____

_____

_____

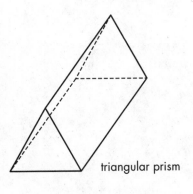

triangular prism

_____

_____

_____

_____

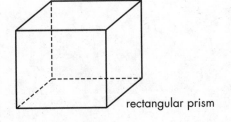

rectangular prism

_____

_____

_____

_____

# To the Family

## Identifying Geometric Shapes in the Real World

*Session 1*

**Math Content**

Identifying three-dimensional shapes in the real world

**Materials**

Student Sheet 1

Pencil

Magazines, catalogs, newspapers (optional)

In class, we have been exploring and sorting a set of three-dimensional shapes. For homework, your child will find real objects that look like the solid geometric shapes pictured on Student Sheet 1. Your child can look for examples in and around your house (for example, a paper towel tube is a cylinder), as well as in magazines, catalogs, and newspapers. Your child will cut out or sketch examples and bring them to school.

# Building Triangles

Build the triangles described below. Draw a picture of each triangle you build. Label the length of each stick you use.

---

**1.** Make a triangle with all sides the same length.

**2.** Make a triangle with all sides different lengths.

---

**3.** Can you find three sticks that will **not** make a triangle? If you can, draw them. Label them to show their lengths. Why won't these sticks make a triangle?

---

**Optional**

How many different triangles can you build using one 5-inch stick, one 6-inch stick, and one 8-inch stick? Draw them on the back of this sheet.

# Building Squares

1. Build two different squares. Draw a picture of each square. Label the length of each side.

2. Can you build a square with one 6-inch stick, one 5-inch stick, one 4-inch stick, and one 3-inch stick? Why or why not?

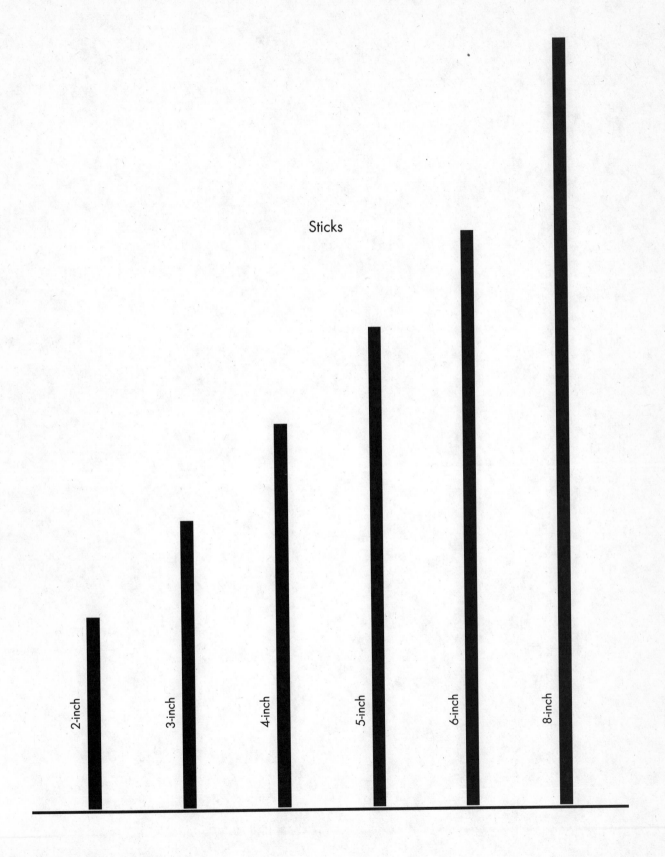

Sticks

2-inch  3-inch  4-inch  5-inch  6-inch  8-inch

# Building Rectangles

**1.** Build three different rectangles. Draw a picture of each rectangle. Label the lengths of the sides.

**2.** Can you build a rectangle with one 5-inch stick, one 6-inch stick, and two 3-inch sticks? Why or why not?

**Optional**
How many different four-sided polygons can you build using one 8-inch stick, one 6-inch stick, one 5-inch stick, and one 4-inch stick? Draw some of them on the back of this sheet. Be sure to label the lengths of the sides.

# Finding Polygons at Home

Find several examples of polygons at home.
List or draw them below.

◺ Triangles

```



```

▫ Squares

```



```

▭ Rectangles

```



```

# To the Family

## Finding Polygons at Home

*Sessions 1–2*

**Math Content**
Identifying two-dimensional shapes in the real world

**Materials**
Student Sheet 5
Pencil
Ruler
Magazines, catalogs, newspapers (optional)

In class, we have been building two-dimensional polygons (such as squares, rectangles, and triangles) and exploring how the length of sides affects shape. For homework tonight, your child will find real-world examples of the 2-D shapes she or he made in school today, paying particular attention to the length of sides, and will record or tape examples on the student sheet.

# Geometric Solids

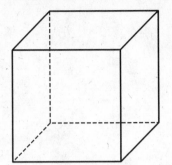

cube

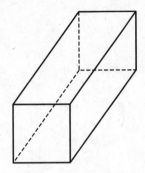

square prism

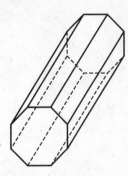

octagonal prism

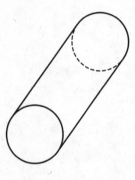

cylinder

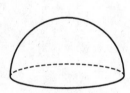

hemisphere

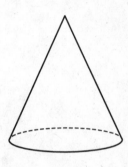

cone

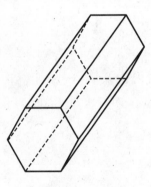

hexagonal prism

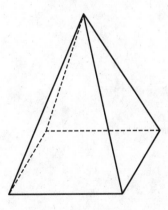

square pyramid

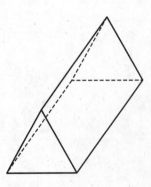

triangular prism

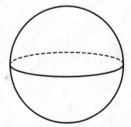

sphere

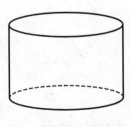

cylinder

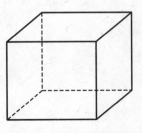

rectangular prism

# 2-D Quick Images at Home

1. Cut out the Quick Images below.

2. The "chooser" picks a shape and displays it for 3 seconds.

3. The "drawer" tries to draw the shape from the image in his or her mind.

4. Repeat steps 2 and 3 using the same shape so that the drawer can revise the drawing.

5. The chooser reveals the shape and compares it to the drawing. How did you see the image on successive flashes? How did you remember what the shape looked like?

| Shape 1 | Shape 2 |
|---|---|
| Shape 3 | Shape 4 |
| Shape 5 | Shape 6 |

# To the Family

## 2-D Quick Images at Home

*Session 3*

**Math Content**
Organizing and analyzing visual images

**Materials**
Student Sheet 7
Pencil
Paper
Scissors

In class, we have been spending some time (about 10 minutes each
time) doing an activity called Quick Images. In this activity, students are
shown a picture of a geometric image for three seconds and then try to
draw or create it from memory. This gives children experience organizing and analyzing visual images and an opportunity to develop concepts
and language needed to reflect on and communicate about spatial
relationships. Tonight for homework, your child will do the activity
with someone at home.

# Geometric Solids

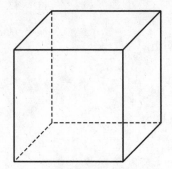

cube

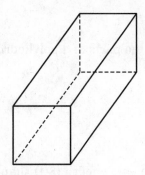

square prism

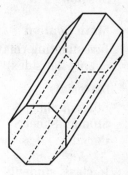

octagonal prism

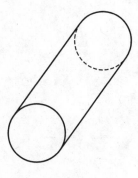

cylinder

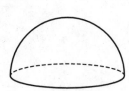

hemisphere

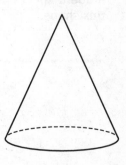

cone

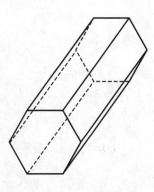

hexagonal prism

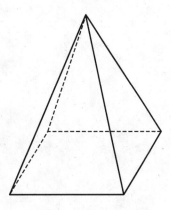

square pyramid

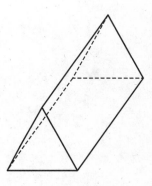

triangular prism

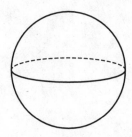

sphere

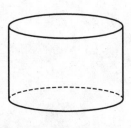

cylinder

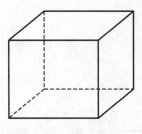

rectangular prism

# To the Family

## Writing Descriptions

*Sessions 4–5*

### Math Content
Investigating relationships among the parts of a polyhedron (shapes with only flat sides)

### Materials
Student Sheet 6
Student Sheet 8
Pencil

In class, students have been building polyhedra (3-D shapes with flat sides) by looking at pictures and by listening to verbal directions and descriptions. For homework, your child will choose a polyhedron from Student Sheet 6 and write on Student Sheet 8 directions for building this shape.

# Writing Descriptions

1. Choose a secret polyhedron (a shape with flat sides only) from the shapes on Student Sheet 6.

2. Write the name of the polyhedron you choose on the back of this sheet.

3. Write directions that would help someone build your polyhedron.

For example: My polyhedron has exactly 6 square faces. (My secret polyhedron is a cube.)

# To the Family

## Writing Descriptions

*Sessions 4–5*

**Math Content**
Investigating relationships among the parts of a polyhedron (shapes with only flat sides)

**Materials**
Student Sheet 6
Student Sheet 8
Pencil

In class, students have been building polyhedra (3-D shapes with flat sides) by looking at pictures and by listening to verbal directions and descriptions. For homework, your child will choose a polyhedron from Student Sheet 6 and write on Student Sheet 8 directions for building this shape.

# Patterns for Cube Boxes

Which of these patterns do you think can be used to make an open box for a cube? Write YES by the letter if you think a pattern will make a box. Write NO if you think it won't make a box. Cut out the patterns to check your predictions.

**Predictions**

A. _____ B. _____ C. _____ D. _____ E. _____

# Home Box Pattern

Find a small box that you can unfold or cut apart.

What does the box usually hold?

When the box is unfolded, I think the pattern will look like this:

When I unfolded my box, the pattern looked like this:

# To the Family

## Home Box Pattern

*Session 1*

**Math Content**
Relating three-dimensional geometry (a box) to two-dimensional
  geometry (the same box unfolded)
Visualizing and predicting

**Materials**
Student Sheet 10
A box
Paper
Pencil

In class, students have been exploring 2-D patterns that fold to make
3-D shapes. Tonight for homework, your child will be doing the reverse:
exploring a 3-D shape that unfolds to make a 2-D geometric pattern.
Your child will find a small box and predict what the box will look like
when it is unfolded. Then he or she will unfold the box and record the
results on Student Sheet 10.

# More Patterns

**1.** Make a pattern for an open box
that holds two 1-inch cubes.
Use graph paper.
Find as many patterns as you can.

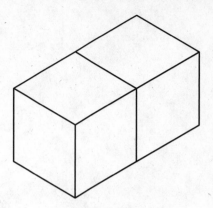

**2.** Use triangle paper to make patterns for a four-sided pyramid.
All of its sides should look like the
triangle below.

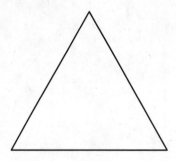

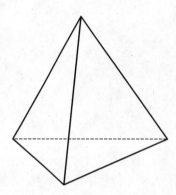

Your pyramid can be any size.
Find as many patterns as you can.

four-sided pyramid

# TRIANGLE PAPER

# To the Family

## More 2-Cube Box Patterns

*Session 2*

**Math Content**
Exploring two-dimensional geometric patterns that fold to make
three-dimensional shapes
Improving visualization skills

**Materials**
Graph paper
2 cubes (optional)
Pencil
Scissors

In class, students have been using graph paper to design patterns that
will make open boxes (boxes with no tops or lids) to hold two cubes.
Each pattern has to follow these rules: It has to be made from a single
piece of paper; it can be folded only along the edges of the squares; and
no sides can overlap. For example, if you were to cut out the following
pattern and fold along the dark lines, you would have an open box that
holds two cubes exactly.

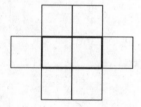

There are many possible patterns. Tonight for homework, your child will
use graph paper to continue designing patterns that fold into boxes that
hold two cubes exactly.

# To the Family

## More 2-Cube Box Patterns
*Session 2*

### Math Content
Exploring two-dimensional geometric patterns that fold to make three-dimensional shapes
Improving visualization skills

### Materials
Graph paper
2 cubes (optional)
Pencil
Scissors

In class, students have been using graph paper to design patterns that will make open boxes (boxes with no tops or lids) to hold two cubes. Each pattern has to follow these rules: It has to be made from a single piece of paper; it can be folded only along the edges of the squares; and no sides can overlap. For example, if you were to cut out the following pattern and fold along the dark lines, you would have an open box that holds two cubes exactly.

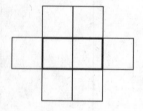

There are many possible patterns. Tonight for homework, your child will use graph paper to continue designing patterns that fold into boxes that hold two cubes exactly.

# To the Family

## More 2-Cube Box Patterns

*Session 2*

**Math Content**

Exploring two-dimensional geometric patterns that fold to make
  three-dimensional shapes
Improving visualization skills

**Materials**

Graph paper
2 cubes (optional)
Pencil
Scissors

In class, students have been using graph paper to design patterns that
will make open boxes (boxes with no tops or lids) to hold two cubes.
Each pattern has to follow these rules: It has to be made from a single
piece of paper; it can be folded only along the edges of the squares; and
no sides can overlap. For example, if you were to cut out the following
pattern and fold along the dark lines, you would have an open box that
holds two cubes exactly.

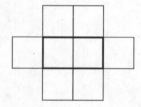

There are many possible patterns. Tonight for homework, your child will
use graph paper to continue designing patterns that fold into boxes that
hold two cubes exactly.

# How Many Cubes? (page 1 of 4)

Pattern A makes a rectangular box without a top.
How many cubes do you predict will fit in the box? _____

To check your answer, cut out the pattern, build the
box, and fill the box with cubes.

Name _____  Date _____

**Student Sheet 12**

# How Many Cubes? (page 2 of 4)

Pattern B makes a rectangular box without a top.
How many cubes do you predict will fit in the box? _____

To check your answer, cut out the pattern, build the
box, and fill the box with cubes.

B

*Investigation 4 • Session 1*
*Exploring Solids and Boxes*

# How Many Cubes? (page 3 of 4)

Pattern C makes a rectangular box without a top.
How many cubes do you predict will fit in the box? _____

To check your answer, cut out the pattern, build the
box, and fill the box with cubes.

C

# How Many Cubes? (page 4 of 4)

Pattern D makes a rectangular box without a top.
How many cubes do you predict will fit in the box? _____

To check your answer, cut out the pattern, build the box, and fill the box with cubes.

D

## Optional
Make some patterns for boxes that contain exactly 15 cubes.

# THREE-QUARTER-INCH GRAPH PAPER

# THREE-QUARTER-INCH GRAPH PAPER

# Boxes That Hold 12 Cubes

Use graph paper to design a pattern that is different from the one below. Your pattern should make a box to hold this solid. Your box does not need a top or lid.

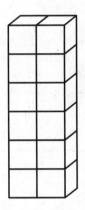

You should be able to cut out the pattern you design and fold it up into a box that will hold this solid.

Here is an example:

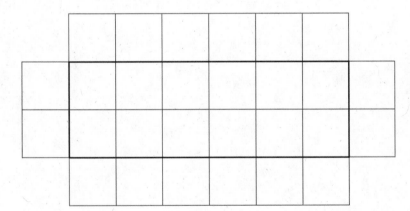

*Investigation 4 • Session 2*
*Exploring Solids and Boxes*

# To the Family

## Boxes That Hold 12 Cubes

*Session 2*

**Math Content**
Designing patterns for a box to hold 12 cubes

**Materials**
Student Sheet 13
Graph paper

In class, students have been designing patterns for open rectangular boxes that will hold exactly 12 cubes linked together. There are many possible patterns that would make a box to hold these cubes. (See the example on Student Sheet 13.) Tonight for homework, your child will use graph paper to find several patterns that work.

*Unit Resource*
*Exploring Solids and Boxes*

# THREE-QUARTER-INCH GRAPH PAPER

**75**

# Making Boxes from the Bottom Up (page 1 of 3)

**1.** The dark squares make the bottom of
a rectangular box that contains exactly
6 cubes. The box has no top. Draw the
sides to finish the pattern for the box.

# Making Boxes from the Bottom Up (page 2 of 3)

2. The dark squares make the bottom of
a rectangular box that contains exactly
9 cubes. The box has no top. Draw the
sides to finish the pattern for the box.

# Making Boxes from the Bottom Up (page 3 of 3)

**3.** The dark squares make the bottom of
a rectangular box that contains exactly
8 cubes. The box has no top. Draw the
sides to finish the pattern for the box.

© Dale Seymour Publications®

*Investigation 4 • Session 3*
*Exploring Solids and Boxes*

# An 18-Cube Box Pattern

The dark squares make the bottom of
a rectangular box that contains exactly
18 cubes. The box has no top. Draw the
sides to finish the pattern for the box.

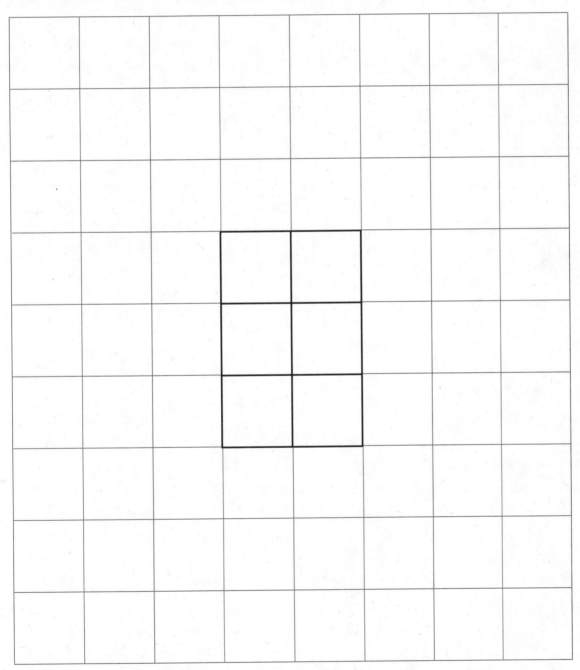

How did you figure out your pattern for this box?
Write your answer on the back of this sheet.

# A 16-Cube Box Pattern

The dark squares make the bottom of a rectangular box that contains exactly 16 cubes. The box has no top. Draw the sides to finish the pattern for the box.

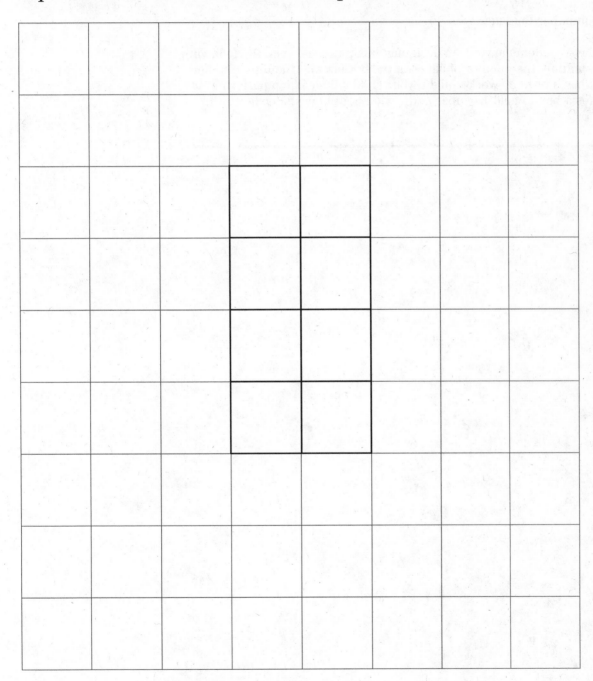

How did you figure out your pattern for this box?
Write your answer on the back of this sheet.

# To the Family

## A 16-Cube Box Pattern

*Session 3*

**Math Content**
Designing patterns for a box to hold 16 cubes

**Materials**
Student Sheet 16
Graph paper (optional)

In class, students have been designing box patterns given the following information: the number of cubes in the bottom and the total number of cubes. For homework tonight, your child will design a pattern that makes a box to hold 16 cubes and write about how she or he did it.

# THREE-QUARTER-INCH GRAPH PAPER

# THREE-QUARTER-INCH GRAPH PAPER

# THREE-QUARTER-INCH GRAPH PAPER

**THREE-QUARTER-INCH GRAPH PAPER**

**93**

*Unit Resource*
*Exploring Solids and Boxes*

# THREE-QUARTER-INCH GRAPH PAPER

# THREE-QUARTER-INCH GRAPH PAPER

# THREE-QUARTER-INCH GRAPH PAPER

**101**

# THREE-QUARTER-INCH GRAPH PAPER

**103**

# THREE-QUARTER-INCH GRAPH PAPER

# THREE-QUARTER-INCH GRAPH PAPER

*Unit Resource*
*Exploring Solids and Boxes*

# THREE-QUARTER-INCH GRAPH PAPER

# Box City Riddles

**1.** I am building a box that holds a 12-cube solid. The bottom layer (or floor) has 4 cubes in it. How many layers (or floors) will I have in my building? How do you know?

**2.** I am building a mall that has 3 floors. Each floor has 5 cubes in it. How many cubes will I have in my mall? How did you figure this out?

**3.** I am building a skyscraper with 12 floors. I have 36 cubes altogether inside my skyscraper. How many cubes are in each floor? How do you know?

**4.** On the back of this sheet, make up your own riddle.

# To the Family

## Box City Riddles

*Sessions 1–4*

**Math Content**

Solving problems using addition, subtraction, multiplication
and/or division

**Materials**

Student Sheet 17
Pencil
Objects for counting (optional)

In class, students have been planning and building a city made from
three-dimensional boxes (without tops or lids). They have also been predicting and then computing the total number of connected cubes that
will fill a "building." Tonight for homework, your child will solve similar
problems using any operation (addition, subtraction, multiplication
and/or division) that makes sense to them.

# Mystery Solids

Find the total number of cubes that would fill each
open box exactly. Write the number in the center of the
pattern. You might cut and fold the patterns to check.

**1.**

**2.**

# To the Family

## Mystery Solids

*Sessions 1–4*

### Math Content
Visualizing how a two-dimensional box pattern folds into a
   three-dimensional box
Predicting

### Materials
Student Sheet 18
Pencil

In class, we have continued to plan and build our cities. Tonight for homework, your child will predict how many cubes would fit in a given box pattern once it is made into a box. Your child might want to cut out each pattern and fold it into a box to help think about the problem and/or to double check and compare original predictions.

# The Arranging Chairs Puzzle

## What You Will Need

30 small objects to use as chairs (for example, cubes, blocks, tiles, chips, pennies, buttons)

## What to Do

1. Choose a number greater than 30.

2. Figure out all the ways you can arrange that many chairs. Each row must have the same number of chairs. Your arrangements will make rectangles of different sizes.

3. Write down the dimensions of each rectangle you make.

4. Choose another number and start again. Be sure to make a new list of dimensions for each new number.

### Example
All the ways to arrange 12 chairs

**Dimensions**
1 by 12
12 by 1
2 by 6
6 by 2
3 by 4
4 by 3

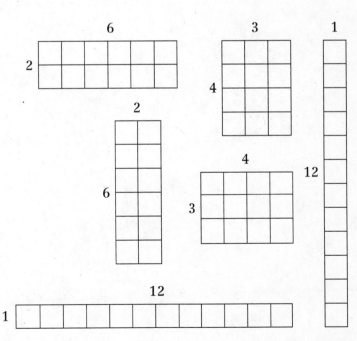

## Practice Page A

Solve this problem in two different ways, and write about how you solved it:

**216 + 98 =**

Here is the first way I solved it:

Here is the second way I solved it:

# Practice Page B

Solve this problem in two different ways, and write about how you solved it:

256 + 124 =

Here is the first way I solved it:

Here is the second way I solved it:

**119**

## Practice Page C

I bought 5 half-gallons of milk. From each half-gallon I can get 8 glasses of milk. How many glasses of milk will I have altogether?

Show how you solved this problem. You can use numbers, words, or pictures.

## Practice Page D

My sister runs around the track five times a week. Each time she goes, she runs 16 laps. How many laps does she run each week?

Show how you solved this problem. You can use numbers, words, or pictures.

# Practice Page E

We have 120 stickers that we want to sell at our garage sale. We will put 12 stickers in each bag to sell. How many bags of stickers will we have?

Show how you solved this problem. You can use numbers, words, or pictures.